THE FIRST HOUR

Very early in the morning, while it was still dark,
Jesus got up, left the house and went off to a
Solitary place where he prayed.

MARK 1:35

BILLY
God Bless

EPH 6:11

THE FIRST HOUR – 30-Day Study Guide By: Mark W. Koch

PRESENTED TO:

_____

FROM:

_____

DATE:

_____

THE FIRST HOUR MISSION

To train men to become everything God
Intended Them to be...Godly Men—
Fathers—Leaders; Equipping them to
Spread the message of Jesus Christ
Throughout the world.

Searched...Fed...Led!

The first hour of every day has been the most meaningful, challenging, yet the most glorious Hour of my day for the past 40 years. The first thing I do every morning is fall to my knees in Prayer and repentance. We sin everyday, hence I start my day in prayer reflecting on the past 24 hours so that I can confess what needs to be confessed. What a joy it is to know that His forgiveness is guaranteed. After prayer, I read the Word of God. Once I have done this, I am a vessel ready to be led by the Spirit. My first hour is meaningful because I meet with God, it is challenging because the Word of God will convict me when I have missed the mark, and it is glorious because of His forgiveness and the confident assurance that I will be led each day by His Spirit. I endorse and recommend wholeheartedly The First Hour for Men, as it is precisely what I have been doing for many years.

Coach Bill McCartney
Founder, Promise Keepers

I spent 20 years in the Army living each day in strict obedience to the Army regulation. I did well in the Army as a direct result of my obedience to the Army regulation. I gave my life to Jesus my last year in the military and realized immediately that I had a new regulation – The Bible. I immediately began to live my life in strict adherence to the Word of God in the same way that I obeyed the Army regulation. My spiritual maturity increased rapidly. Then I met Coach Mac, a man of prayer, who would not answer a question without asking for divine guidance. It revolutionized my life. For the last 20 years, as direct result of Coach's influence on my life, my first hour of every day is governed by being Searched, Fed and Led by the Spirit. "The First Hour for Men Study Guide is truly God's tool that will transform and equip men to be Godly men who are daily led by the Spirit of the Living God."

Raleigh B. Washington, DD, M. Div
President/CEO, Promise Keepers

Foreword *by* **Rich DeVos**

It's not easy for many men to humble themselves before God. We've been brought up to be tough on the playing fields, not to cry, to be heads of households, bread winners and hard-nosed businessmen. We don't like stopping for directions, let alone asking someone for help.

We pride ourselves on being self-made, but we're really God-made. He knows our hearts better than we know ourselves. And only God knows the plan He has for our lives. So why wouldn't we naturally turn to our Father in Heaven to ask for guidance?

The First Hour makes it simple. Just one hour a day that will change your life and help you to seek God first.

I've built very successful businesses, so some people might view me as self-sufficient and in control. But I realize everything I have and everything I am is by the grace of God. So, before tackling business and facing the demands of the day, I face God. It is there, without distraction, where, as a husband, as a father and as a man, I can appreciate all the blessings I've been given and evaluate the ways in which I'm using those gifts.

In these pages Mark gives all men a step-by-step outline to spending a fulfilling hour a day with God. From spiritual enlightenment, to career development, to strengthening their marriage, to their own self worth, there isn't a fundamental area of a man's life that cannot be improved by following this 30-day study guide.

Richard M. DeVos, Sr.

THE MISSION

"Restoring God's America"

America is at a crossroads. For the last 100 years our traditional Judeo/Christian values have been slowly and methodically eroded to the point that our founding fathers' vision for "One Nation Under God" is hardly recognizable. Prayer has been removed from our schools, the Ten Commandments have been removed from our courtrooms and most importantly God has been removed as the head of our households. We are on a rapid descent into a Godless society where massive Government replaces spirituality in the lives of everyday Americans.

However, we believe that the main reason for this moral decay, is because "We The People" have veered away from the Godly principles this country was founded on.

It's America's men that have lost their own integrity and morals throughout the decades and have set an ungodly, poor example, to their children and families. In order to turn this country around and begin the process of restoring this Nation, we must first turn its men around and begin to heal them.

The First Hour for men is a simple, effective tool that is making a major impact in the process of restoring America back to "One Nation Under God."

The First Hour is uniting Godly men in America to become prayer warriors that are committing to changing themselves, their family and ultimately this nation through prayer and a pledge to their patriotic duty. We believe:

If You Heal The Man... He Will Heal His Family...
The Family Will Heal The Nation!

1. HEAL THE MAN

We must first bring America's men back to a closer "Daily Relationship" with God. The evil forces that are destroying this Nation are a direct result of men, the head of the household, living in disobedience and ignoring God's Commandments. Without the men in this country first changing themselves, the family does not stand a chance and America is destined for continual destruction.

"The First Hour" for men, is accomplishing the goal of restoring the man back to a closer daily relationship with God. Our goal is to distribute One Million copies throughout the U.S. by year end 2024. To date, over 300,000 books have been shipped to men across the Nation. Why One Million?

We need at least one million men to be a tipping point for lasting change. We encourage these men to make three commitments.

First - Commit to completing the 30-Day Journey. Testimonies are pouring in and miracles of restoration are happening in the lives of men and their families who are committing to and completing this 30-Day Journey.

Second - Commit to all 7 steps of the First Hour program, which will result in dramatic changes in all areas of their life.

Third - Commit to share this book with four other men. We will encourage each man to make a solid commit to give away four books. Two books to fellow believers to keep the momentum going, and two books to men that they believe do not have a personal relationship with Jesus Christ. This will continue to duplicate and create a grass roots movement throughout the nation and inspire a movement of the Holy Spirit that we believe will make a difference for generations to come.

2. HEAL THE FAMILY

Once the Man turns back to a solid daily relationship with God and returns to his role as the spiritual head of the household, he will then consciously and unconsciously begin to heal his family by providing a positive, Godly example. The First Hour is assisting in this process by providing men with the tools and educational materials to begin to restore and lead their family. The restoration of the American family is the key to restoring our founding father's dream of a government that is "Of the People, By the People and For the People," under the direction of God.

3. HEAL THE NATION

With millions of men praying each morning, we can begin the process of changing this Nation back into the God-fearing, traditional value system that our founding father's designed.

The final step to continue the process of healing this Nation is to encourage all the First Hour partners and their families to make a "Solid Commitment" to their "Patriotic Duty" and vote. We will call on them to Vote in every single election from here on out. From the county school boards, to the local judges, the mayor, the governor and every single local, state and National election. No matter what their political party affiliation, they must vote for the candidates who respect the Constitution and the Godly Principles upon which this great Nation was founded on.

We will encourage and challenge every man in this Nation to get back to a closer daily relationship with God. We will challenge them to become the spiritual leader of their homes, we will challenge them to become the man, the father and the husband that God intended them to be. We will challenge them to rise up and vote for the Godly politicians that share the same moral principals and values that they do.

And lastly, we will challenge them to share the message of salvation through a personal relationship with Jesus Christ. If we all join together and do our part in the Great Commission... we can make an impact to help restore this nation.

United in God We Stand, Divided We Fall. *With God's help and our commitment, America can return to **"One Nation Under God."***

God Bless You... And God Bless America!

Mark W. Koch

THE FIRST HOUR
The Story Behind the Study

You are about to begin what I believe will be the best thirty days you will ever experience in your life. It's no coincidence that you have this book in your hands right now. There is no doubt in my mind that this is a Divine appointment!

As you read how The First Hour began, I hope you will be convinced that I had nothing to do with the creation of this study guide. This is God's message to you; it was developed by Him, not me. I truly believe that I was just chosen to put it on paper for you. I know that's a pretty bold statement; it might even sound arrogant, but believe me, God has humbled me many times over. What I am trying to say is... this devotion is a gift from "God to You". I take no credit for it. My background is pretty simple. I had a dream, pursued it, and accomplished it. I was a big shot Hollywood producer, so I thought. I broke some box office records with my film Lost in Space, made a lot of money, achieved all of my worldly dreams, was at the top of my game, and was totally miserable. With a broken marriage, an ego the size of Manhattan and truly "lost in space", I cried out to God. He answered, stripped me down to nothing, took all my worldly possessions, remolded me, and lifted me back up, but this time for His glory.

So here's how the story goes. It may seem far-fetched to you, maybe a bit crazy, or just a series of coincidences, but I challenge you to seek God with the same passion that I did, ask Him to give you signs for yourself, and then make your determination. I believe He will answer you in the same way He did me.

First, I want to explain how God revealed all the information for me to write down in this study. God speaks to people in many different ways. It is very common for people to say that God spoke to my spirit, God spoke to my heart, or God spoke to me in a dream. God spoke to me in a very simple way; He spoke to my mind. I am convinced that He made my thoughts agreeable to His will. The ideas that would come into my mind to write down for this study would just come out of nowhere. I had no premeditated plan to develop a study guide for men. In fact, I had no desire to do this at all. I am convinced that the Holy Spirit guided me through each simple step for me to share with you.

You are truly blessed, because God has chosen you to get to know Him more intimately through these next thirty days. Your life is about to change...drastically!

Early one morning in July of 2004, I woke up suddenly, rolled over in bed, and looked at my alarm clock. The bright digital numbers read 5:55 a.m. I didn't have a bad dream or hear any loud noise. The reason this was so unusual was because I am not a morning person; I never have been one of those people that can get out of bed early in the morning. I have always been a night owl, working until at least midnight and most of the time into the wee hours of the night. It was God who woke me up at 5:55 a.m. that morning. As I looked at the clock and laid back down to go to sleep, over and over in my mind the same thought kept agonizing me, "Give God your first waking hour every morning for the next thirty days; a half hour of prayer and a half hour of reading His Word." The thought kept racing through my mind! Get up, go pray, and read the Bible. I kept fighting it, trying to go back to sleep, but I was wide-awake. God allowed me no choice in the matter. I felt the presence of the God like I have never felt before. Two things just kept repeating themselves over and over in my mind... get up and go pray for a half hour, and read the Bible for a half hour. Give Me the first hour of every day for the next thirty days. I could not even think about anything else. Finally, I got out of bed and headed upstairs. I kept saying to myself, thirty minutes of prayer? What was I going to pray about for thirty minutes? I can pretty much ask God for everything I need in five minutes or less. I went upstairs to my desk and sat down. I kept thinking to myself, thirty minutes of prayer, that's a long time!

As I sat down at my desk, right smack in the middle of it was the book, Prayers That Avail Much by Germaine Copeland. It was given to my wife as a birthday gift from her friend; she must have put it on my desk knowing I was the one that needed the prayers. "Perfect!" I said to myself. "I will just go through the contents page and pick out some prayers that I feel pertain to me and my needs and start praying as many of them as I can until thirty minutes is up." That's exactly what I did. I went through the table of contents and started to pick prayers randomly. I was going from prayers on page 174 to page 42 back to page 257 to page 72 and so on. I had no particular order. I thought I was just choosing the prayers that just came into my mind. What I didn't realize at the time was that God had a plan. He was leading me in a particular order.

After thirty minutes sharp, I stopped and picked up my Bible. I knew that God wanted me to read a half hour of His Word. What part of the Bible should I read for thirty minutes? What came to my mind instantly was the book of Proverbs and The New Testament. The book of Proverbs was perfect because there are 31 chapters, and I had committed to 30 days. Each chapter was approximately a page to a page and a half, and would only take a couple of minutes. The next thing I did was look in my Bible and see how many pages were in the New Testament— there were two hundred and forty in my NIV version. Two hundred and forty divided by thirty days was only 8 pages a day. I said to myself, "If I only read 4 pages a day front and back, I will read the entire New Testament in 30 days." The next thing God revealed to me was that I was to learn The Ten Commandments ... inside out... upside down ... and from the middle! When I finished, I had five minutes left over. I then asked God what to do with the last five minutes, and what instantly came to my mind was close your eyes and listen to Me.

To make sure I read the prayers in the same order each day, I attached yellow sticky notes the very first day and numbered the order of the prayers. After the first week, I was getting tired of jumping around from all the different pages in the book, and the sticky notes were starting to fall off, so I decided to have my assistant type up the prayers in the order that I was praying them each day. When she finished retyping them, she printed them out and handed them to me. She looked as white as a ghost. She said, "Do you see what I see? It's what my Pastor always says, God first, family second, career third." I looked through the freshly typed sheets, and sure enough, the first several prayers all pertained to God, the second set pertained to family, and the third pertained to career. I did not plan this. I believe this is a message from God to you on how He wants you to set your priorities in life. They were in perfect order. As you know, our God is a God of perfect order. It is not a coincidence that the order just happened to come out that way. I can assure you that this was truly Divine intervention.

After the first couple of days, I asked my wife if she would make up a 30-day chart on her computer for me to check off my assignments. The second she handed me the chart, I immediately wrote down seven things that I wanted to accomplish in the 30-day period. There was no thought about it. It was automatic... the seven steps just came to my mind and flew through me. I just recently learned that the number seven is a very important Biblical number, it Means COMPLETION!

By the end of the third week, people were noticing a drastic change in me; they noticed a certain peace about me that they had not seen before. They began asking me what I was doing differently. I just had to share it. I was getting up at 5:55 every morning and giving my First Hour to God, and I'd never felt this great in my entire life. My assistant came to me and said, "You need to put this in a simple course for everyone who is asking what you are doing." She wanted her husband to start it immediately.

I spent the next two days in my office putting the 30-day program together for a few friends. I never understood why I was driven to make it so clear and important that they should memorize the Ten Commandments for ten days straight and then write them over and over again until they were hammered into their heads. It was so elementary. I mean after the first ten days of repeating them, a first grader could have memorized them. As you read on, you will see the significance of this.

Throughout the next several months, I still had no intention of making this a book to be available to the general public. It was something that I put together only to share with a few of my friends, not realizing that God had other plans. This is when God confirmed to me, in his own way, that He had other plans to bring this material to the world. It was almost comical. Everywhere I looked, the number 555 came up. For the next several months, at least once or twice a week, 555 appeared to me in the craziest places. Here are just a few of the examples.

Numerous times after I finished my first hour with God, I turned the television on and as soon as I turned it on, I heard the Domino's 555 commercial. "555 just 555. Three pizzas for just $5.55 each." I saw this ad everywhere, on Billboards, newspapers, I heard it on the radio over and over. It was a huge campaign for them and it hounded me for months.

I went to the doctor to schedule my eye surgery. They gave me the date: April 27, 2005. They called me on April 24th and told me they were going to have to reschedule my appointment for the following week. On May 5th, the day of my appointment, I showed up for my surgery. As they handed me the fifteen different release documents to sign, each time I signed my name, I had to date it. As I dated the very first signature, I realized... here we go again, May 5, 2005, which of course, I abbreviated, 05-05-05. I just laughed, but I was starting to understand that God had a message for me regarding the 555. It was getting ridiculous. It was way beyond coincidental. My airline flight that I have been taking to L.A. for 6 years always departed at 6:15. They changed it to 5:55. I took my wife's car into Firestone to get new tires, on the work order they put 555 in two separate places. Under the license number it said 555-FL and under mileage they put 555 miles. Obviously that is not her tag number or the mileage of the car. He was probably just too busy to go check the tag and mileage. I kept the work order and will frame it as a reminder. I could go on and on as to how many times the numbers appeared to me, but I don't want to bore you. However, I do have to give you one more example that put the icing on the cake for me.

I was in Miami at a delicatessen and I sat down to have lunch by myself. I ordered a turkey sandwich and a bottle of water, even though I really wanted a Mountain Dew. I'd been trying to change my drinking habits. When my turkey sandwich arrived, I bowed my head to pray. With so many different things going on in my life at this particular time, my prayer was very simple. "Lord, it seems that I'm going in so many directions right now. Please show me your will for my life and reveal to me what you want me to focus my time on." At least, three separate times during lunch, the waitress passed me with a can of Mountain Dew, delivering each of them to other customers. Finally, the pressure was too much.

I caved in. I was down to the last couple of bites of my sandwich and I waved the waitress over. I told her that I couldn't stand it any longer! "Bring me a can of Mountain Dew!" She laughed and brought me the Mountain Dew. She also picked my bill up and recalculated it, adding the 90 cents more for the Mountain Dew. What do you suppose the bill came out to then? Five dollars and fifty-five cents—$5.55! I said, "OK Lord. I get it. I will focus on this 30-Day Study for men."

During the same time as all of the 555 messages, the Ten Commandments also kept popping up everywhere. Judge Roy Moore just happened to be in the news at the time that I was designing the pages for the study to give to friends. Out of the blue, he called me personally and asked me to get involved in his fight to help him keep the country's focus on the laws of the founding Fathers of our nation, specifically, The Ten Commandments. He was ordered to remove The Ten Commandments monument from the State Supreme Court building. It was all over the news channels and press for several weeks. He wanted me to make a movie about it. A few days later I had a project offered to me to do a remake of the film "The Decalogue." I didn't even know what that word meant. When I asked my partner about it, he told me it was a project about the Ten Commandments. When I went to church that Sunday, my pastor announced that over the next ten weeks he would be doing a study on... you guessed it... the Ten Commandments. Again, I could go on and on, just as I was hounded by the 555 message, I was equally hounded by signs of the Ten Commandments. I think you get the message of what God was trying to get through my thick skull here. He wanted to make sure I would include the Commandments in this course and reveal to you how important they are to Him. After all, they are His laws.

I got the message, came up with the title Tender Warriors 5:55, designed the book and printed up five hundred of them. As you begin this study, and read through the prayers, you will see that the sixth prayer that I have been praying for a couple of months during this time was, "To Walk in God's Wisdom and His Perfect Will." The first sentence says, "Father, I ask You to give me a complete understanding of what You want to do in my life..." and it goes on later to say, "I roll my works upon You, Lord, and You make my thoughts agreeable to Your will..." All of these revelations of the 555 shouldn't be such a surprise to me... or to you. After all, I'd been praying every morning for several months for God to reveal His will for my life. God always answers the prayers of those who diligently seek Him, and I know as you begin your journey of giving your First Hour to God, He will reveal His will for your life as well. Don't be surprised if the number 555 starts popping up all over the place. It has happened to many men who have started this course.

Finally, after these books started circulating to all of my friends, the meaning of 555 was revealed to me. A good friend of mine, Dean Lovett, came to my office. As soon as he picked up the book and looked at the title, he questioned me on the number 555 and what the meaning of that was. I explained to him all the 555 messages God has hounded me with and that I was convinced it was the time he wanted me and YOU to get up each morning and spend the First Hour with Him. He said, "Mark, everyone is not going to get up at 5:55. That couldn't have been His purpose. There has to be some other reason for it." He asked me if I had gone through The Bible and found any Scripture that is relevant with those numbers involved. I told him I had researched it extensively and I could not find any chapter 5, verse 55 in any of the books.

Dean was so troubled by it, that he was completely driven to figure it out.

He searched the entire Bible, searching to see if there was another reason besides getting up at 5:55 in the morning for this number. He was so bothered by it that he actually pulled over to the side of the road after leaving my office and frantically searched his Bible. He was getting ready to close the book because he couldn't find it anywhere. Then God spoke to him. What instantly came into his mind was to check the 5th book, 5th chapter and 5th verse. He went to the fifth book, which is Deuteronomy and went to the fifth chapter; the heading was in bold black and said: "THE TEN COMMANDMENTS." He then went to the fifth verse, which by the way is in parentheses, and says: "AT THAT TIME I stood between the Lord and you to declare to you the word of the Lord." Dean called me on the phone, barely able to talk, and said, " Go get your Bible and go to Deuteronomy, which is the fifth book, go to the fifth chapter and read the fifth verse." When I looked it up, chills ran through my body. I finally had the answer to what 555 meant. I believe with all my heart, God is using me as a vessel to share and reconfirm His message of the Ten Commandments.

As I continued to pray the prayers each morning and spend time with God for the next several months, something else very important was revealed to me. Besides the Ten Commandments, there is another message that I believe God gave to me to share with you:

The three key factors to powerful and effective prayer.

There is no coincidence that these are the first three prayers in the prayer section of the book. God laid on my heart the word W.A.R. We are in a spiritual battle and the "Three Key Daily Steps" to prepare for this battle are as follows:

W: Wash yourself with the precious blood of Jesus Christ and repent, this gives you a fresh start each day.

A: Armor up! Put on the full armor of God so that you will be able to stand up to everything the Enemy throws your way.

R: Refill yourself with the Holy Spirit each day.

These first three prayers have radically transformed thousands of men's prayer lives."

The first prayer is to ask for forgiveness and repentance.

God's ears are closed to an unclean heart and spirit. You must first ask God to forgive you for all of the sins from the previous day (don't we all have some), and you must truly repent and ask God to forgive you. What God was revealing to me was that He will hear our prayers, but He will not listen to them or answer them unless we pray to Him with a freshly renewed and clean spirit. I did some research on this and sure enough, this is what I found in the Bible:

"It's your sins that have cut you off from God. Because of your sins, He has turned away and will not listen anymore." - Isaiah 59:2

Why should we bother confessing our sins to God when we pray? Isaiah's words should send a chill up our spines, "Because of your sins, He has turned away and will not listen anymore."

Sin... unconfessed sin... has a way of dulling God's ears to our prayers!

When there's something wicked and sinful buried in our hearts, God doesn't pretend that everything is OK. He is determined that we deal with it before moving forward with the plans He has for us.

When we ask God to forgive us and cover our sins with the Blood of Jesus Christ and we truly mean it, all of our sins are forgiven. Now not only are you Righteous through Christ, but at that time each morning, you stand sinless before the throne of God.

The second prayer is to put on the Armor of God each morning.

"God is strong, and He wants you strong. So take everything the Master has set out for you, well-made weapons of the best materials, and put them to use so you will be able to stand up to everything the Devil throws your way." Ephesians 6:10-11

Although we seldom realize it, we're always wrestling against the unseen powers in the spiritual realm. There's an unending struggle and prayer is the weapon that will turn the tide. "Stay alert. Watch out for your great enemy, the Devil. He prowls around like a roaring lion, looking for someone to devour." - 1 Peter 5:8

Satan will do whatever he can to keep you from praying and communicating with God, because he knows you are completely helpless against him on your own. But when we approach the devil on praying ground, in the mighty strength of the Lord, we stand in a strength that's superior to the devil in every way. He wants to keep that weapon out of our hands!

It's interesting that God's Word compares the devil to a lion. When a lion catches its prey, it will often use its powerful jaws to clamp down on the mouth of its unfortunate victim. It does this so its prey can't cry out for help from the rest of its herd. That's Satan's strategy against us. He wants to keep us quiet, to keep us from prayer, because he knows the armies of heaven are at our call.

The third prayer is to ask for a fresh refilling of the Holy Spirit.

Jesus said, "If you then, though you are evil, know how to give good gifts to your children, how much more will your Father in heaven give the Holy Spirit to those who ask him!" - Luke 11:13 and Acts 1:8 says "But you will receive power when the Holy Spirit comes on you; and you will be my witnesses in Jerusalem, and in all Judea and Samaria, and to the ends of the earth."

You now have the three keys to powerful and effective prayer; it's as simple as one, two, three! Ask Him for forgiveness, put on your armor, and pray for a fresh refilling of the Holy Spirit. You are now ready to approach the throne of our Almighty God.

God has a plan for your life. He's your Father and you're His son. He wants a father and son relationship with you. He wants you to be successful. He can't help you unless you let Him. He will discipline you. He will ground you. He will also lift you up. However, you need to follow His rules. You have to strive for obedience!

Obedience = Blessings... Disobedience = Discipline... it's that simple!

As I was writing this letter to you, many times I tried to dig into Scripture and make this as intelligent as I could. Yet the more I tried to add Scripture and stories from the Bible to try to validate my message to you, the more I would just get discouraged and end up back at square one. I would always go back to just writing from the heart, writing from what I truly believe was coming from God, not me. The message that God kept putting into my mind was K.I.S.S. "Keep It Simple Son." I am not a theologian, nor am I a Bible scholar. As a matter of fact, most of you reading this right now probably know Scripture a lot better than I do.

The reason I believe that God is using me, is because I am one of His children that is just an average "C" student at best. Therefore, the message is simple. I will not try to teach you anything. God will reveal everything He wants you to know over the next thirty days. I believe I was just chosen to share with you the three keys to powerful, effective prayer and a life' changing experience when you earnestly seek Him with all your heart and make Him first in your life.

In Conclusion, this book gives you the opportunity to start fresh each day. It gives you the chance to really get to know your Heavenly Father and have a true relationship with Him. It gives you the opportunity to be all that He wants you to be and experience the life He has planned for you. He has a destiny for you, and a perfect plan for your life. Spend time with Him each day, pray to Him, love Him, seek Him, and ask Him to help you to be the son He wants you to be. Strive for obedience, and watch Him change, mold, and use you in a way you could have never imagined. He loves you. LOVE HIM! Talk to Your Father each and every morning until you finally meet Him face to face.

The time is now! Get up tomorrow morning and begin your new journey and watch the blessings start pouring in. I know that God will show you the same thing that He showed me as you start your first hour each morning with Him.

The prayers in this study guide are powerful and will change you from the inside out. They will reveal God's will for you, guide you through each day, and affect every area of your life.

May God Bless You Abundantly,

Mark W. Koch

The First Hour Commitment

I believe that you are about to begin what will be the most incredible 30-day journey of your life! I truly believe that this book is a gift from God to you. It's now in your hands and I pray that you will make a solid decision to follow the three commitments below.

COMMITMENT 1

I commit to giving God my first hour each morning for the next thirty days by completing "The First Hour" 30-day journey.

COMMITMENT 2

I commit to follow all of the seven simple steps (page 22) that make up the First Hour 30-day program.

COMMITMENT 3

When I experience "Dramatic Changes" in my life after completing The First Hour, I commit to doing my part in "The Great Commission" by sharing The First Hour for Men with a minimum of four other men; two fellow Christian brothers and two men that I feel do not have a personal relationship with Jesus Christ.

I hereby agree to keep the above three commitments.

Signature:_____

The First Hour Objectives

By the end of this 30-day journey, and if you earnestly seek God with all your heart each morning, I am convinced that you will experience the following:

- YOU WILL have developed a more intimate relationship with your Heavenly Father, His Son Jesus Christ, and the Holy Spirit.

- YOU WILL have a more clear and better understanding of God's will and purpose for your life.

- YOU WILL have achieved a closer relationship with your wife, your children and your friends.

- YOU WILL have attained a higher self-esteem.

- YOU WILL feel healthier and be more physically fit.

- YOU WILL be on your way to becoming the man God intended you to be.

Daily Devotionals

As you start your 30-day journey, "Make Sure" you sign up for the daily devotionals / messages from Mark. They will be sent to your email each morning. Simply scan the QR code below to sign up!

The Seven Simple Steps

Follow these seven simple steps and watch God show up and begin to make drastic changes in your life! The Blessings are about to begin as you make this commitment.

1. WAKE UP TIME - God wants you to rise early each day. Set a time and stick to it. This needs to be uninterrupted time. By giving your first waking hour to God in prayer, your entire day will improve. He wants to be involved in even the smallest details throughout your day.

2. MORNING PRAYERS - 30 Minutes – Prayer is the most powerful weapon you have! God Promises to answer the prayers of the righteous according to His will. Pray the prayers in this book "In Order" each day and do not skip any of them. Some people find it helpful, especially during the first few days, to read out loud. [morning prayers begin on page 87]

3. BIBLE READING – 30 Minutes - God's Word is alive! It is our rule book and manual for everyday life. By reading just 25 minutes a day, you will have read the entire New Testament and the Book of Proverbs by the end of this course! Save the last five minutes to relax and listen to God.

4. WORKOUT - This is a crucial part of the program. God wants you to take care of your body. If you already have a work out regime, then stick to it. I encourage you to get a minimum of 15-minutes of exercise each day. You will feel and see the difference in 30-days!

5. RETURN HOME - It is important to be consistent with the time you come home. Your family needs the security of a consistent leader.

6. TIME WITH CHILDREN - 1/2 hr. Minimum, Plus Bedtime Prayer - It is important that you devote quality time each day to your children. The power of the word "Dad" reaches beyond a youngster's childhood. In fact, it spans for generations. Commit to this quality time and you will see a drastic improvement in your children and in your relationship with them.

7. TIME WITH WIFE - 1 hr. Minimum, Plus Bedtime Prayer - Commit to a minimum of one hour of quality time each day with your wife. Pray each night with her. This may be uncomfortable at first, so start out with just a very short prayer. Each night will get easier, and God will take over. Remember a couple that prays together...stays together. **You will see an unbelievable improvement in your Marriage and in your relationship with your wife!**

DAY 1

Make a commitment to get up at the same time each morning. Put an **X** in the **Yes** box if you were successful or an **X** in the **No** box if you were not. Then write in the **actual** time. Continue to do the same process with the remaining six steps.

Proverbs 6:9-11
"How long will you lie there, you sluggard? When will you get up from your sleep? A little sleep, a little slumber, a little folding of the hands to rest, and poverty will come on you Like a bandit and scarcity like an armed man."

ACTION		YES	NO	ACTUAL
1. Wake up time	_____ a.m.			
2. Morning Prayers	30 Minutes *(page 87)*			
3. Bible Reading	30 Minutes			
A. Proverbs Chapter 1	5 Minutes			
B. New Testament, Matthew 1	20 Minutes			
C. Listening to God	5 Minutes			
4. Workout	15 minutes *(min.)*			
5. Return Home	Goal: _____			
6. Time with Children	30 Minutes *(+ bedtime prayer)*			
7. Time with Wife	1 Hour (+ bedtime prayer)			

The Ten Commandments *(Memorize)*

1. You shall have no other gods before Me.

DAY 2

He holds victory in store for the upright, He is a shield to those whose walk is blameless, for He guards the course of the just and protects the way of His faithful ones.

PROVERBS 2:7-8

IMPORTANT!

Use this journal space on each day to record significant events as they happen. Expect to see things happen in your life. Record your experiences, events, feelings, and confirmations each day. Jot down your experiences during prayer time, your relationship with your wife, changes in your children, or other differences you notice. Some days you will have nothing to write. Other days you will run out of space. You may not be used to writing things down, but I encourage you to give it a try. Your journal will create a permanent reminder of God's work during your 30-Day Journey!

If you choose, read at your own pace. God may slow you down to dwell on certain scriptures He wants you to really study and learn. **Do NOT put pressure on yourself to finish within the 30-day time period!** It's all about spending your first hour with God. This is a 30-Day commitment, for some it may not be 30-Days in a row.

J O U R N A L

Write it down!

ACTION		YES	NO	ACTUAL
1. Wake up time	_____ a.m.			
2. Morning Prayers	30 Minutes *(page 87)*			
3. Bible Reading	30 Minutes			
A. Proverbs Chapter 2	5 Minutes			
B. New Testament	20 Minutes			
C. Listening to God	5 Minutes			
4. Workout	15 minutes *(min.)*			
5. Return Home	Goal: _____			
6. Time with Children 30 Minutes *(+ bedtime prayer)*				
7. Time with Wife	1 Hour *(+ bedtime prayer)*			

The Ten Commandments *(Memorize)*

1. You shall have no other gods before Me.
2. You shall not make for yourself an idol.

DAY 3

My son, do not forget My teaching, but keep My Commands in your heart, for they will prolong your life many years and bring you prosperity. Let love and faithfulness never leave you. Bind them around your neck, write them on the tablet of your heart, then you will win favor and a good name in the sight of God and man.

PROVERBS 3:1-4

J O U R N A L

ACTION		YES	NO	ACTUAL
1. Wake up time	_____ a.m.			
2. Morning Prayers	30 Minutes *(page 87)*			
3. Bible Reading	30 Minutes			
A. Proverbs Chapter 3	5 Minutes			
B. New Testament	20 Minutes			
C. Listening to God	5 Minutes			
4. Workout	15 minutes *(min.)*			
5. Return Home	Goal: _____			
6. Time with Children 30 Minutes *(+ bedtime prayer)*				
7. Time with Wife	1 Hour (+ bedtime prayer)			

The Ten Commandments *(Memorize)*

1. You shall have no other gods before Me.
2. You shall not make for yourself an idol.
3. You shall not take the Lord's name in vain.

DAY 4

Put away perversity from your mouth; keep corrupt talk far from your lips. Let your eyes look straight ahead, fix your gaze directly before you.

PROVERBS 4:24-25

JOURNAL

ACTION		YES	NO	ACTUAL
1. Wake up time _____ a.m.				
2. Morning Prayers 30 Minutes *(page 87)*				
3. Bible Reading 30 Minutes				
A. Proverbs Chapter 4 5 Minutes				
B. New Testament 20 Minutes				
C. Listening to God 5 Minutes				
4. Workout 15 minutes *(min.)*				
5. Return Home Goal: _____				
6. Time with Children 30 Minutes *(+ bedtime prayer)*				
7. Time with Wife 1 Hour *(+ bedtime prayer)*				

The Ten Commandments *(Memorize)*

1. You shall have no other gods before Me.

2. You shall not make for yourself an idol.

3. You shall not take the Lord's name in vain.

4. Remember the Sabbath day by keeping it holy.

DAY 5

For a man's ways are in full view of the Lord;
and he examines all his paths. The evil deeds
of a wicked man ensnare him; the cords of
his sin hold him fast. He will die for lack of
discipline led astray by his own great folly.

PROVERBS 5:21-23

JOURNAL

ACTION		YES	NO	ACTUAL
1. Wake up time	_____ a.m.			
2. Morning Prayers	30 Minutes *(page 87)*			
3. Bible Reading	30 Minutes			
A. Proverbs Chapter 5	5 Minutes			
B. New Testament	20 Minutes			
C. Listening to God	5 Minutes			
4. Workout	15 minutes *(min.)*			
5. Return Home	Goal: _____			
6. Time with Children 30 Minutes *(+ bedtime prayer)*				
7. Time with Wife	1 Hour (+ bedtime prayer)			

The Ten Commandments *(Memorize)*

1. You shall have no other gods before Me.
2. You shall not make for yourself an idol.
3. You shall not take the Lord's name in vain.
4. Remember the Sabbath day by keeping it holy.
5. Honor your father and your mother.

DAY 6

> But a man who commits adultery lacks judgment; whoever does so destroys himself. Blows and disgrace are his lot, and his shame will never be wiped away.
>
> PROVERBS 6:32-33

JOURNAL

ACTION		YES	NO	ACTUAL
1. Wake up time _____ a.m.				
2. Morning Prayers 30 Minutes *(page 87)*				
3. Bible Reading 30 Minutes				
A. Proverbs Chapter 6 5 Minutes				
B. New Testament 20 Minutes				
C. Listening to God 5 Minutes				
4. Workout 15 minutes *(min.)*				
5. Return Home Goal: _____				
6. Time with Children 30 Minutes *(+ bedtime prayer)*				
7. Time with Wife 1 Hour *(+ bedtime prayer)*				

The Ten Commandments *(Memorize)*

1. You shall have no other gods before Me.
2. You shall not make for yourself an idol.
3. You shall not take the Lord's name in vain.
4. Remember the Sabbath day by keeping it holy.
5. Honor your father and your mother.
6. You shall not murder.

DAY 7

My son, keep My words and store up My commands within you. Keep My commands and you will live; guard My teachings as the apple of your eye.

PROVERBS 7:1-2

JOURNAL

You should have completed reading up to Luke, Chapter 3 of the New Testament. If you have not, dedicate extra time when you have it to get caught up. **However, this is only if you have the goal to complete the entire New Testament in 30-days.**

Do NOT put pressure on yourself to finish within the 30-day time period! This is a 30-Day commitment, for some it may not be 30-Days in a row.

ACTION		YES	NO	ACTUAL
1. Wake up time	_____ a.m.			
2. Morning Prayers	30 Minutes *(page 87)*			
3. Bible Reading	30 Minutes			
A. Proverbs Chapter 7	5 Minutes			
B. New Testament	20 Minutes			
C. Listening to God	5 Minutes			
4. Workout	15 minutes *(min.)*			
5. Return Home	Goal: _____			
6. Time with Children 30 Minutes *(+ bedtime prayer)*				
7. Time with Wife	1 Hour (+ bedtime prayer)			

The Ten Commandments *(Memorize)*

1. You shall have no other gods before Me.
2. You shall not make for yourself an idol.
3. You shall not take the Lord's name in vain.
4. Remember the Sabbath day by keeping it holy.
5. Honor your father and your mother.
6. You shall not murder.
7. You shall not commit adultery.

DAY 8

Now then, My sons, listen to Me. Blessed are those who keep My ways. Listen to My instruction and be wise. Do not ignore it. Blessed is the man who listens to Me, watching daily at My doors, waiting at My doorway. For whoever finds Me, finds life and receives favor from the Lord.

PROVERBS 8:32-35

JOURNAL

ACTION		YES	NO	ACTUAL
1. Wake up time	_____ a.m.			
2. Morning Prayers	30 Minutes *(page 87)*			
3. Bible Reading	30 Minutes			
A. Proverbs Chapter 8	5 Minutes			
B. New Testament	20 Minutes			
C. Listening to God	5 Minutes			
4. Workout	15 minutes *(min.)*			
5. Return Home	Goal: _____			
6. Time with Children 30 Minutes *(+ bedtime prayer)*				
7. Time with Wife	1 Hour (+ bedtime prayer)			

The Ten Commandments *(Memorize)*

1. You shall have no other gods before Me.
2. You shall not make for yourself an idol.
3. You shall not take the Lord's name in vain.
4. Remember the Sabbath day by keeping it holy.
5. Honor your father and your mother.
6. You shall not murder.
7. You shall not commit adultery.
8. You shall not steal.

DAY 9

The fear of the Lord is the beginning of wisdom, and knowledge of the Holy One is understanding, for through Me, your days will be many, and years will be added to your life.

PROVERBS 9:10-11

JOURNAL

ACTION		YES	NO	ACTUAL
1. Wake up time _____ a.m.				
2. Morning Prayers 30 Minutes *(page 87)*				
3. Bible Reading 30 Minutes				
A. Proverbs Chapter 9 5 Minutes				
B. New Testament 20 Minutes				
C. Listening to God 5 Minutes				
4. Workout 15 minutes *(min.)*				
5. Return Home Goal: _____				
6. Time with Children 30 Minutes *(+ bedtime prayer)*				
7. Time with Wife 1 Hour *(+ bedtime prayer)*				

The Ten Commandments *(Memorize)*

1. You shall have no other gods before Me.
2. You shall not make for yourself an idol.
3. You shall not take the Lord's name in vain.
4. Remember the Sabbath day by keeping it holy.
5. Honor your father and your mother.
6. You shall not murder.
7. You shall not commit adultery.
8. You shall not steal.
9. You shall not give false testimony against your neighbor.

DAY 10

Ill-gotten treasures are of no value,

but righteousness delivers from death. The Lord does not let the righteous go hungry, but He thwarts the craving of the wicked.

PROVERBS 10:2-3

JOURNAL

ACTION		YES	NO	ACTUAL
1. Wake up time	_____ a.m.			
2. Morning Prayers	30 Minutes *(page 87)*			
3. Bible Reading	30 Minutes			
A. Proverbs Chapter 10	5 Minutes			
B. New Testament	20 Minutes			
C. Listening to God	5 Minutes			
4. Workout	15 minutes *(min.)*			
5. Return Home	Goal: _____			
6. Time with Children 30 Minutes *(+ bedtime prayer)*				
7. Time with Wife 1 Hour (+ bedtime prayer)				

The Ten Commandments *(Memorize)*

1. You shall have no other gods before Me.
2. You shall not make for yourself an idol.
3. You shall not take the Lord's name in vain.
4. Remember the Sabbath day by keeping it holy.
5. Honor your father and your mother.
6. You shall not murder.
7. You shall not commit adultery.
8. You shall not steal.
9. You shall not give false testimony against your neighbor.
10. You shall not covet your neighbor's wife.

DAY 11

One man gives freely, yet gains even more; another withholds unduly, but comes to poverty. A generous man will prosper; he who refreshes others will himself be refreshed.

PROVERBS 11:24-25

JOURNAL

ACTION		YES	NO	ACTUAL
1. Wake up time	_____ a.m.			
2. Morning Prayers	30 Minutes *(page 87)*			
3. Bible Reading	30 Minutes			
A. Proverbs Chapter 11	5 Minutes			
B. New Testament	20 Minutes			
C. Listening to God	5 Minutes			
4. Workout	15 minutes *(min.)*			
5. Return Home	Goal: _____			
6. Time with Children	30 Minutes *(+ bedtime prayer)*			
7. Time with Wife	1 Hour (+ bedtime prayer)			

The Ten Commandments *(Write them)*

1. _____

DAY 12

No harm befalls the righteous, but the wicked have their fill of trouble. The Lord detests lying lips, but He delights in men who are truthful.

PROVERBS 12:21-22

JOURNAL

ACTION		YES	NO	ACTUAL
1. Wake up time	_____ a.m.			
2. Morning Prayers	30 Minutes *(page 87)*			
3. Bible Reading	30 Minutes			
A. Proverbs Chapter 12	5 Minutes			
B. New Testament	20 Minutes			
C. Listening to God	5 Minutes			
4. Workout	15 minutes *(min.)*			
5. Return Home	Goal: _____			
6. Time with Children 30 Minutes *(+ bedtime prayer)*				
7. Time with Wife	1 Hour *(+ bedtime prayer)*			

The Ten Commandments *(Write them)*

1. _____

2. _____

DAY 13

Misfortune pursues the sinner, but prosperity is the reward of the righteous. A good man leaves an inheritance for his children's children, but a sinner's wealth is stored up for the righteous.

PROVERBS 13:21-22

JOURNAL

ACTION		YES	NO	ACTUAL
1. Wake up time	_____ a.m.			
2. Morning Prayers	30 Minutes *(page 87)*			
3. Bible Reading	30 Minutes			
A. Proverbs Chapter 13	5 Minutes			
B. New Testament	20 Minutes			
C. Listening to God	5 Minutes			
4. Workout	15 minutes *(min.)*			
5. Return Home	Goal: _____			
6. Time with Children 30 Minutes *(+ bedtime prayer)*				
7. Time with Wife	1 Hour (+ bedtime prayer)			

The Ten Commandments *(Write them)*

1. _____

2. _____

3. _____

DAY 14

He who fears the Lord has a secure fortress,
And for his children, it will be refuge. The fear
of the Lord is a fountain of life, turning a man
from the snares of death.

PROVERBS 14:26-27

JOURNAL

You should have completed reading up to Acts, Chapter 3 of the New Testament. If you have not, dedicate extra time when you have it to get caught up. **However, this is only if you have the goal to complete the entire New Testament in 30-days.**

ACTION		YES	NO	ACTUAL
1. Wake up time _____ a.m.				
2. Morning Prayers 30 Minutes *(page 87)*				
3. Bible Reading 30 Minutes				
A. Proverbs Chapter 14 5 Minutes				
B. New Testament 20 Minutes				
C. Listening to God 5 Minutes				
4. Workout 15 minutes *(min.)*				
5. Return Home Goal: _____				
6. Time with Children 30 Minutes *(+ bedtime prayer)*				
7. Time with Wife 1 Hour *(+ bedtime prayer)*				

The Ten Commandments *(Write them)*

1. _____

2. _____

3. _____

4. _____

DAY 15

The Lord detests the sacrifice of the wicked, but the prayer of the upright pleases Him. The Lord detests the way of the wicked, but He loves those who pursue righteousness. Stern discipline awaits him who leaves the path; he who hates correction will die.

PROVERBS 15:8-10

JOURNAL

ACTION		YES	NO	ACTUAL
1. Wake up time	_____ a.m.			
2. Morning Prayers	30 Minutes *(page 87)*			
3. Bible Reading	30 Minutes			
A. Proverbs Chapter 15	5 Minutes			
B. New Testament	20 Minutes			
C. Listening to God	5 Minutes			
4. Workout	15 minutes *(min.)*			
5. Return Home	Goal: _____			
6. Time with Children 30 Minutes *(+ bedtime prayer)*				
7. Time with Wife	1 Hour (+ bedtime prayer)			

The Ten Commandments *(Write them)*

1. _____

2. _____

3. _____

4. _____

5. _____

DAY 16

Commit to the Lord whatever you do, and your plans will succeed. The Lord works out everything for His own ends-even the wicked for a day of disaster.

PROVERBS 16:3-4

JOURNAL

ACTION		YES	NO	ACTUAL
1. Wake up time	_____ a.m.			
2. Morning Prayers	30 Minutes *(page 87)*			
3. Bible Reading	30 Minutes			
A. Proverbs Chapter 16	5 Minutes			
B. New Testament	20 Minutes			
C. Listening to God	5 Minutes			
4. Workout	15 minutes *(min.)*			
5. Return Home	Goal: _____			
6. Time with Children 30 Minutes *(+ bedtime prayer)*				
7. Time with Wife	1 Hour *(+ bedtime prayer)*			

The Ten Commandments *(Write them)*

1. _____

2. _____

3. _____

4. _____

5. _____

6. _____

DAY 17

A man of knowledge uses words with restraint, and a man of understanding is even-tempered.

PROVERBS 17:27

JOURNAL

ACTION		YES	NO	ACTUAL
1. Wake up time	_____ a.m.			
2. Morning Prayers	30 Minutes *(page 87)*			
3. Bible Reading	30 Minutes			
A. Proverbs Chapter 17	5 Minutes			
B. New Testament	20 Minutes			
C. Listening to God	5 Minutes			
4. Workout	15 minutes *(min.)*			
5. Return Home	Goal: _____			
6. Time with Children 30 Minutes *(+ bedtime prayer)*				
7. Time with Wife 1 Hour (+ bedtime prayer)				

The Ten Commandments *(Write them)*

1. _____

2. _____

3. _____

4. _____

5. _____

6. _____

7. _____

DAY 18

The name of the Lord is a strong tower; the righteous run to it and are safe. The heart of the discerning acquires knowledge; the ears of the wise seek it out.

PROVERBS 18:10,15

JOURNAL

ACTION		YES	NO	ACTUAL
1. Wake up time	_____ a.m.			
2. Morning Prayers	30 Minutes *(page 87)*			
3. Bible Reading	30 Minutes			
A. Proverbs Chapter 18	5 Minutes			
B. New Testament	20 Minutes			
C. Listening to God	5 Minutes			
4. Workout	15 minutes *(min.)*			
5. Return Home	Goal: _____			
6. Time with Children 30 Minutes *(+ bedtime prayer)*				
7. Time with Wife	1 Hour *(+ bedtime prayer)*			

The Ten Commandments *(Write them)*

1. _____
2. _____
3. _____
4. _____
5. _____
6. _____
7. _____
8. _____

DAY 19

Listen to advice and accept instruction, and in the end you will be wise. Many are the plans in a man's heart; but it is the Lord's purpose that prevails. Stop listening to instruction, My son, and you will stray from the words of knowledge.

PROVERBS 19:20-21, 27

JOURNAL

ACTION		YES	NO	ACTUAL
1. Wake up time	_____ a.m.			
2. Morning Prayers	30 Minutes *(page 87)*			
3. Bible Reading	30 Minutes			
A. Proverbs Chapter 19	5 Minutes			
B. New Testament	20 Minutes			
C. Listening to God	5 Minutes			
4. Workout	15 minutes *(min.)*			
5. Return Home	Goal: _____			
6. Time with Children 30 Minutes *(+ bedtime prayer)*				
7. Time with Wife	1 Hour (+ bedtime prayer)			

The Ten Commandments *(Write them)*

1. _____
2. _____
3. _____
4. _____
5. _____
6. _____
7. _____
8. _____
9. _____

DAY 20

> Do not love sleep, or you will grow poor; stay
> awake and you will have food to spare.
>
> PROVERBS 20:13

JOURNAL

ACTION		YES	NO	ACTUAL
1. Wake up time	_____ a.m.			
2. Morning Prayers	30 Minutes *(page 87)*			
3. Bible Reading	30 Minutes			
A. Proverbs Chapter 20	5 Minutes			
B. New Testament	20 Minutes			
C. Listening to God	5 Minutes			
4. Workout	15 minutes *(min.)*			
5. Return Home	Goal: _____			
6. Time with Children 30 Minutes *(+ bedtime prayer)*				
7. Time with Wife	1 Hour (+ bedtime prayer)			

The Ten Commandments *(Write them)*

1. _____
2. _____
3. _____
4. _____
5. _____
6. _____
7. _____
8. _____
9. _____
10. _____

DAY 21

> He who pursues righteousness and love finds
> life, prosperity and honor.
>
> PROVERBS 21:21

JOURNAL

You should have completed reading up to 2 Corinthians, Chapter 2 of the New Testament. If you have not, dedicate extra time when you have it to get caught up.

ACTION		YES	NO	ACTUAL
1. Wake up time	_____ a.m.			
2. Morning Prayers	30 Minutes *(page 87)*			
3. Bible Reading	30 Minutes			
A. Proverbs Chapter 21	5 Minutes			
B. New Testament	20 Minutes			
C. Listening to God	5 Minutes			
4. Workout	15 minutes *(min.)*			
5. Return Home	Goal: _____			
6. Time with Children 30 Minutes *(+ bedtime prayer)*				
7. Time with Wife	1 Hour *(+ bedtime prayer)*			

Matthew 18:19-20

Again, I tell you that if two of you on earth agree about anything you ask for, it will be done for you by My Father in heaven. For where two or three come together in My name, there am I with them.

DAY 22

Train a child in the way he should go, and when he is old he will not turn from it.

PROVERBS 22:6

J O U R N A L

ACTION		YES	NO	ACTUAL
1. Wake up time	_____ a.m.			
2. Morning Prayers	30 Minutes *(page 87)*			
3. Bible Reading	30 Minutes			
A. Proverbs Chapter 22	5 Minutes			
B. New Testament	20 Minutes			
C. Listening to God	5 Minutes			
4. Workout	15 minutes *(min.)*			
5. Return Home	Goal: _____			
6. Time with Children 30 Minutes *(+ bedtime prayer)*				
7. Time with Wife	1 Hour (+ bedtime prayer)			

Proverbs 15:8-9

The Lord detests the sacrifice of the wicked, but the prayer of the upright pleases him. The Lord detests the way of the wicked but He loves those who pursue righteousness.

DAY 23

Do not wear yourself out to get rich; Have the wisdom to show restraint. Cast but a glance at riches, and they are gone, for they will surely sprout wings and fly off to the sky like an eagle.

PROVERBS 23:4-5

JOURNAL

ACTION		YES	NO	ACTUAL
1. Wake up time	_____ a.m.			
2. Morning Prayers	30 Minutes *(page 87)*			
3. Bible Reading	30 Minutes			
A. Proverbs Chapter 23	5 Minutes			
B. New Testament	20 Minutes			
C. Listening to God	5 Minutes			
4. Workout	15 minutes *(min.)*			
5. Return Home	Goal: _____			
6. Time with Children 30 Minutes *(+ bedtime prayer)*				
7. Time with Wife	1 Hour *(+ bedtime prayer)*			

Mark 11:24-26

Therefore, I tell you, whatever you ask for in prayer, Believe that you have received it, and it will be yours. And when you stand praying, if you hold anything against anyone, forgive him, so that your Father in Heaven may forgive you your sins.

DAY 24

By wisdom a house is built and through understanding It is established; through knowledge its rooms are filled with rare and beautiful treasures.

PROVERBS 24:3-4

JOURNAL

ACTION		YES	NO	ACTUAL
1. Wake up time	_____ a.m.			
2. Morning Prayers	30 Minutes *(page 87)*			
3. Bible Reading	30 Minutes			
A. Proverbs Chapter 24	5 Minutes			
B. New Testament	20 Minutes			
C. Listening to God	5 Minutes			
4. Workout	15 minutes *(min.)*			
5. Return Home	Goal: _____			
6. Time with Children 30 Minutes *(+ bedtime prayer)*				
7. Time with Wife	1 Hour (+ bedtime prayer)			

Philippians 4:6-7

Do not be anxious about anything, but in everything, by prayer and petition, with thanksgiving, present your requests to God. And the peace of God, which transcends all understanding, will guard your hearts and your minds in Christ Jesus.

DAY 25

> Like a city whose walls are broken down, is a
> man who lacks self-control.
>
> PROVERBS 25:28

JOURNAL

ACTION		YES	NO	ACTUAL
1. Wake up time	_____ a.m.			
2. Morning Prayers	30 Minutes *(page 87)*			
3. Bible Reading	30 Minutes			
A. Proverbs Chapter 25	5 Minutes			
B. New Testament	20 Minutes			
C. Listening to God	5 Minutes			
4. Workout	15 minutes *(min.)*			
5. Return Home	Goal: _____			
6. Time with Children 30 Minutes *(+ bedtime prayer)*				
7. Time with Wife	1 Hour *(+ bedtime prayer)*			

James 5:15-16

And the prayer offered in faith will make the sick well; The Lord will raise him up. If he has sinned, he will be forgiven. Therefore confess your sins to each other and pray for each other so that you may be healed. The prayer of a righteous man is powerful and effective.

DAY 26

The words of a gossip are like choice morsels;
they go down to a man's inmost parts.

PROVERBS 26:22

JOURNAL

ACTION		YES	NO	ACTUAL
1. Wake up time	_____ a.m.			
2. Morning Prayers	30 Minutes *(page 87)*			
3. Bible Reading	30 Minutes			
A. Proverbs Chapter 26	5 Minutes			
B. New Testament	20 Minutes			
C. Listening to God	5 Minutes			
4. Workout	15 minutes *(min.)*			
5. Return Home	Goal: _____			
6. Time with Children 30 Minutes *(+ bedtime prayer)*				
7. Time with Wife	1 Hour *(+ bedtime prayer)*			

1 Peter 3:12

For the eyes of the Lord are on the righteous and his ears are attentive to their prayer, but the face of the Lord is against those who do evil.

DAY 27

Be sure you know the condition of your flocks, give careful attention to your herds; for riches do not endure forever, and a crown is not secure for all generations.

PROVERBS 27:23-24

J O U R N A L

ACTION		YES	NO	ACTUAL
1. Wake up time	_____ a.m.			
2. Morning Prayers	30 Minutes *(page 87)*			
3. Bible Reading	30 Minutes			
A. Proverbs Chapter 27	5 Minutes			
B. New Testament	20 Minutes			
C. Listening to God	5 Minutes			
4. Workout	15 minutes *(min.)*			
5. Return Home	Goal: _____			
6. Time with Children 30 Minutes *(+ bedtime prayer)*				
7. Time with Wife	1 Hour *(+ bedtime prayer)*			

1 Chronicles 5:20

They were helped in fighting them, and God handed the Hagrites and all their allies over to them because they cried out to Him during the battle. He answered their prayers, because they trusted in Him.

DAY 28

He who gives to the poor will lack nothing, but he who closes his eyes to them receives many curses.

PROVERBS 28:27

JOURNAL

ACTION		YES	NO	ACTUAL
1. Wake up time	_____ a.m.			
2. Morning Prayers	30 Minutes *(page 87)*			
3. Bible Reading	30 Minutes			
A. Proverbs Chapter 28	5 Minutes			
B. New Testament	20 Minutes			
C. Listening to God	5 Minutes			
4. Workout	15 minutes *(min.)*			
5. Return Home	Goal: _____			
6. Time with Children 30 Minutes *(+ bedtime prayer)*				
7. Time with Wife	1 Hour *(+ bedtime prayer)*			

Deuteronomy 4:7

What other nation is so great as to have their gods near them the way the Lord our God is near us whenever we pray to Him?

DAY 29

> A fool gives full vent to his anger, but a wise man keeps himself under control.
>
> PROVERBS 29:11

JOURNAL

ACTION	YES	NO	ACTUAL
1. Wake up time _____ a.m.			
2. Morning Prayers 30 Minutes *(page 87)*			
3. Bible Reading 30 Minutes			
A. Proverbs Chapter 29 5 Minutes			
B. New Testament 20 Minutes			
C. Listening to God 5 Minutes			
4. Workout 15 minutes *(min.)*			
5. Return Home Goal: _____			
6. Time with Children 30 Minutes *(+ bedtime prayer)*			
7. Time with Wife 1 Hour *(+ bedtime prayer)*			

Matthew 5:44-45

But I say to you, love your enemies and pray for those who persecute you,
So that you may be sons of your Father who is in heaven; for He causes His
sun to rise on the evil and the good, and sends rain on the righteous and the
unrighteous.

DAY 30

ACTION		YES	NO	ACTUAL
1. Wake up time	_____ a.m.			
2. Morning Prayers	30 Minutes *(page 87)*			
3. Bible Reading	30 Minutes			
A. Proverbs Chapter 30	5 Minutes			
B. New Testament	20 Minutes			
C. Listening to God	5 Minutes			
4. Workout	15 minutes *(min.)*			
5. Return Home	Goal: _____			
6. Time with Children 30 Minutes *(+ bedtime prayer)*				
7. Time with Wife	1 Hour *(+ bedtime prayer)*			

Proverbs 31:8-9

Speak up for those who cannot speak for themselves, for the rights of all who are destitute. Speak up and judge fairly; defend the rights of the poor and needy.

Congratulations!

The past 30-days have been a great start to beginning a daily discipline of spending time with God and your family. As you continue your spiritual journey, there are two great callings that God has for you in life. They are explained in the Bible verses below:

THE GREAT COMMANDMENT

*"You must love the Lord your God with all your heart,
All your soul, all your mind, and all your strength. The second
Is equally important: 'Love your neighbor as yourself.'
No other commandment is greater than these."*
Matthew 22:37-40

THE GREAT COMMISSION

*"Then Jesus came to them and said, "All authority in heaven
And on earth has been given to Me. Therefore, go and make
Disciples of all Nations, baptizing them in the name of the Father
And of the Son and of The Holy Spirit, and teaching them to obey
Everything I have commanded you, and surely I am with you
Always, to the very end of the age."*
Matthew 28:18-20

In order to help you strengthen and build on the commitments you have made these past 30-days, take a few moments to read the next two pages and make a covenant and a commitment to continue to live out God's plan for your life by giving Him your first fruits each day.
Tithe Your Time.

The Great Commandment Covenant

LOVING GOD

Today, I make a covenant with God to continue to give Him the first part of my day. I realize that without spending time with Him on a daily basis, I will not be prepared to face the challenges that life brings. I will faithfully continue to read God's Word, pray, and serve Him with everything I have. My goal will be to love God with all my heart. I will also love and serve God by treating my body as His temple.

LOVING OTHERS

Today, I make a covenant with God to love others as I love myself. This will begin with my wife (if married). I will treat her with the love and respect she deserves and strive to be the servant leader God has called me to be in my home. I will also focus on giving my children (if you have children) the love and time that they need so that they will see the example of Christ in me. Finally, I will make a conscious choice to allow Christ's love to flow through me as I come into contact with others on a daily basis.

I _____, enter into this covenant

on this _____ day of _____ , _____.

_____
Signature

The Great Commission Commitment

You have been called by God to join His army and to rise up for this great nation. Your commitment to this program will not only change your life and the lives of your family, but the lives of thousands of other men and their families through your commitment to give this book to four other men, who will in turn share it with four other men, and the cycle will continue to duplicate and sweep the Nation with the message of Jesus Christ!

At the beginning of this book you made three commitments. 1) To following the study guide for the next 30-days. 2) To follow all 7 simple steps of The First Hour program. 3) To do your part in the Great Commission by sharing this book with four other men. Write down the names of two **Christian Brothers** that you feel would benefit from this book. These can be men from your Church, your work, or anyone that you know that already has a personal relationship with Jesus Christ.

1. _____   2. _____

Next, write down the names of **two men that you feel do not have a personal relationship with Jesus Christ.** Pray for God to put these men on your heart! Listen to the Lord and then go and speak to them. Hand them this book and let the Holy Spirit do the rest!

3. _____   4. _____

Please visit **Thefirsthour.com** for additional copies of The First Hour for Men, other books in the First Hour devotional series, related materials and information to support the First Hour mission.

I pray that YOU WILL COMMIT to partner with us and join our fight to continue to spread the message of Jesus Christ throughout this Nation. Join us as an "Outreach Partner" today! **(See next page)**

A Note From the Author

On behalf of the "The First Hour", I am humbled that God has called me to lead such an important mission. To enlist and train men to become the "Husband, Father and Spiritual Leader" of the family that God intended them to be. Equipping them to spread the message of Jesus Christ throughout the Nation.

This Nation is in trouble. We are losing this country. The time is now, we can begin to change the direction of this Nation if we join together and put God back as the head. Below is a scripture that really hit home to me:

"And He said to them, the harvest is plentiful, but the laborers are few. Therefore, pray earnestly to the Lord of the harvest to send out laborers into His harvest." – Luke 10:2

Our goal is to enlist an army "Laborers" of one million men across this Nation. We are committed to give away **One Million books** by the end of 2024. *We can achieve this goal, but we need your commitment!*

Now is the time to meet the enemy at the gates. I invite you to become an "Outreach Partner" and be involved in a movement of The Holy Spirit and an Awakening that I believe with all my heart this country has never seen before. I pray that you will join me and others on this critical mission.

Commit to becoming an Outreach Partner today! Simply go to **TheFirstHour.com** and click on order books, there is an outreach partner opportunity sign up form.

As an outreach partner we ask that you commit to purchase two books per month, *we will pay the cost for two additional free copies and cover the cost of shipping!*

For only $29.90 per month, you can partner with us in the Great Commission and make a huge impact by reaching 4 lost men per month. Make a commitment today to give away one free book a week to a lost brother. We all need to join together and sweep the Nation with the message of Jesus Christ!

God Bless, and may God Bless America!

Mark W. Koch

There's Power in the Hour!

SHARE YOUR TESTIMONY WITH US

Now that you have completed The First Hour, we would love for you to share your testimony. Please go to: **TheFirstHour.com/testimony**

WE WANT TO PRAY FOR YOU

If you are in a need for prayer, please let us pray for you! There is power in Prayer when to or more gather in His Name. Our prayer team is available to you! Please send your prayer requests to: **TheFirstHour.com/prayer**

FOR MORE INFORMATION

For more information on The First Hour 30-Day Journey and to order additional books and resources Please go to: **TheFirstHour.com**

TO ORDER ADDITIONAL COPIES OF THE FIRST HOUR

Scan the QR code

Sinner's Prayer for Salvation

*That if you confess with your mouth Jesus as Lord,
And believe in your heart that God raised Him
From the dead, you will Be saved; for with the heart
A person believes, resulting in Righteousness, and
With the mouth he confesses, resulting in salvation.*
Romans 10:9-10

*Lord Jesus,
I confess I am a sinner and I ask that You forgive me.
I believe that You died on the cross for my sins and
rose again from the dead to give me eternal life. I
ask You to come into my heart. I receive You as my
personal Lord and Savior. Forgive me of all my sins
and wash me clean. Cleanse me with Your Precious
Blood and give me a fresh new start. From this day
forward, I give You control of my life. Lord, make me
the man that You designed me to be. In the name of
Jesus Christ, My Lord and Savior, I pray. Amen.*

Morning Prayers
(30-Minutes Daily)

The Power of Prayer

The prayers in this book are your essential primer for learning how to pray effectively. When you pray according to the Scriptures, you can be assured that you are praying in line with God's will and that He will honor His word. Let these powerful prayers help you discover His best for you, your family, and your career.

Deliberately pray and meditate on each prayer. Allow the Holy Spirit to make the Word a reality in your heart. Your spirit will become alive to God's Word. You will find yourself pouring over His word, hungering for more and more. Remember, the Father promises to reward those who diligently seek Him and promises to answer the prayers of the righteous.

Germaine Copeland
Prayers That Avail Much ®

IMPORTANT

There are 18 prayers in this book. Every prayer has its order and special purpose in preparing you for your day.

Do Not Skip any of the prayers unless they do not pertain to you, (e.g., wife, husband, children, etc.), and **Do Not Switch the Order** of them.

Pray All 18 Prayers Every Day. After a few mornings, you should be able to complete them in 30-minutes or less. Some people find it helpful to read them out loud. Also, make sure to read the Scripture on the **Left Page Every Day.**

CONTENTS

GOD FIRST

FAMILY SECOND

CAREER THIRD

*Anyone who loves their father or mother more than
Me is not worthy of me; anyone who loves
Their Son or daughter more than me is not
Worthy of me. Whoever does not take up their
Cross and follow me Is not worthy of me.
Whoever finds their life will lose it, and
Whoever loses their life for my sake will find it.*

Mathew 10:37-39

GOD
FIRST

Because of the sacrifice of the Messiah,
His blood poured out on the altar of the Cross.
We're a free people—free of penalties and
Punishments, chalked up by all our misdeeds
And not just barely free either; abundantly free!

Ephesians 1:7

To Receive and Walk in Forgiveness

Father, Your Word declares that if I ask for forgiveness, You will forgive and cleanse me from all unrighteousness. Help me to receive forgiveness for my sins. Help me to forgive myself, Father. Your Son, Jesus, said that whatever I ask for in prayer, having faith, and really believing I will receive it according to Your will.

In the face of this feeling of guilt and unworthiness, I receive my forgiveness, and the pressure is gone—my guilt dissolved, my sin disappeared. I am blessed, for You have forgiven my transgressions—You have covered my sins. I get a fresh start, my slate's clean, for You will never count my sins against me or hold anything back from me.

Father, I repent of holding on to bad feelings toward others. I bind myself to Godly repentance and loose myself from bitterness, resentment, envying, strife, and unkindness in any form. I ask Your forgiveness for the sin of _____. By faith, I receive it, having assurance that I am cleansed from all unrighteousness through the body and blood of Jesus Christ. I forgive all who have wronged and hurt me, and ask You to forgive and release them.

I confess Jesus as my Lord and Savior. He has given me the right to become Your child. I acknowledge You, Lord as my Father. Thank You for forgiving me and absolving me of all guilt. I am an overcomer by the blood of the Lamb and by the word of my testimony.

I resist the temptation to be anxious about anything, but in every circumstance and in everything by prayer and petition with thanksgiving continue to make my wants and the wants of others known to God. Whatever I ask for in prayer, I believe it shall be done for me according to His will. In the name of Jesus, Amen.

SCRIPTURE REFERENCES

- 1 John 1:1-10
- Mathew 18:21-35
- Mark 11:25-26

God is strong, and He wants you strong.
So take everything the Master has set out for you,
Well-made weapons of the best materials,
And put them to use so you will be able to stand up
To everything the Devil throws your way.

Ephesians 6:10-11

To Put on the Armor of God

Heavenly Father, I put on the Armor of God with gratitude and praise. You have provided all I need to stand in victory against Satan and his kingdom.

I confidently put on the Belt of Truth. Thank You that Satan cannot stand against the bold use of Truth.

I put on the Breastplate of Righteousness. I embrace that righteousness which is mine by faith in Jesus Christ. I know that Satan must retreat before the righteousness of God.

I put on the Boots of Peace. I claim the peace with God that is mine through justification. I receive the peace of God that touches my emotions and feelings through prayer and sanctification.

Eagerly, Lord, I lift up the Shield of Faith against all the blazing missiles that Satan fires at me. I know that You are my Shield.

I recognize that my mind is a particular target of Satan's deceiving, lustfull, joy robbing ways; I cover my mind with the powerful Helmet of Salvation.

With joy, I lift the Sword of the Spirit, which is the Word of God. I choose to live in its Truth and power. Enable me to use Your Word to defend myself from Satan, and also to wield the Sword well, to push Satan back, to defeat him.

Thank You, dear Lord, for prayer. Help me to keep this Armor well oiled with prayer. All these petitions I ask You through the mighty name of Jesus Christ. Amen.

SCRIPTURE REFERENCES

- Ephesians 6:10-18
- 2 Corinthians 10:4-6
- 2 Corinthians 6:7
- 1 John 4:4
- Psalm 34:14
- Colossians 3:8-14

But you will receive power when the Holy Spirit
Comes on you; and you will be My witnesses
In Jerusalem, and in all Judea and Samaria,
And to the ends of the earth.

Acts 1:8

To Receive the Infilling of the Holy Spirit

My Heavenly Father, I am Your child, for I believe in my heart that Jesus has been raised from the dead, and I have confessed Him as my Lord and Savior.

Jesus said, "How much more shall your Heavenly Father give the Holy Spirit to those who ask Him." I ask You now in the name of Jesus to fill me with the Holy Spirit. I step into the fullness and power that I desire in the name of Jesus. I confess that I am a Spirit-filled Christian. Whatever I ask for in prayer, I believe that it is granted to me, and I will receive it according to your will. In the name of Jesus. Amen.

SCRIPTURE REFERENCES

- John 14:16-17
- Luke 11:13
- Acts 19:1-6
- Acts 1:8
- Acts 2:1-4
- 1 Corinthians 14:2,18,39

Don't grieve God. Don't break His heart.
His Holy Spirit, moving and breathing in you,
Is the most intimate part of your life,
Making you fit for Himself.
Don't take such a gift for granted.

Ephesians 4:30

To Walk in Sanctification

Father, thank You for sanctifying me by the Truth; Your Word is Truth. Jesus, You consecrated Yourself for my sake, so I will be Truth-consecrated in my mission. In the name of Jesus, I repent and turn from my wicked ways. I wash myself and make myself clean. I cease to do evil, and I am learning to do right.

Father, You dwell in me and walk with me. So I leave the corruption and compromise; I leave it for good. You are my Father, and I will not link up with those who would pollute me, because You want me all for Yourself. I purify myself from everything that contaminates body and spirit, perfecting holiness out of reverence for God.

I submit myself to You, Lord—spirit, soul, and body. I strip myself of my old, unrenewed self and put on the new nature, changing whatever needs to be changed in my life. The desire of my heart is to be a vessel unto honor, sanctified, fitting for the Master's use, and prepared for every good work.

Thank You, Lord, that I eat the good of the land, because You have given me a willing and obedient heart. In the name of Jesus. Amen.

SCRIPTURE REFERENCES

- 1 Peter 1:14-16
- John 17:17-19
- Ephesians 4:22-24
- 2 Corinthians 6:17
- Isaiah 1:16-17
- 2 Timothy 2:20-21
- 2 Corinthians 7:1

Open up before God, keep nothing back;
He'll do whatever needs to be done: He'll validate
Your life in the clear light of day, and stamp you with
Approval at high noon. Quiet down before God...
Be prayerful before Him.

Psalm 37:5-7

To Pray

Father, in the name of Jesus, I thank You for calling me to be a joint promoter and a laborer together—with You. I commit to pray and not to give up.

Jesus, You are the Son of God, and I will never stop trusting You. You are my High Priest, and You understand my weaknesses. So I come boldly to the throne of my gracious God. There I receive mercy and find grace to help when I need it.

There are times I do not know what to pray for. Holy Spirit, I submit to Your leadership and thank You for interceding for us with groans that words cannot express. You search hearts and know the mind of the spirit, because You intercede for the saints in accordance with God's will.

You made Christ, Who never sinned, to be the offering for our sin, so that we could be made right with You through Christ. Now my earnest, heartfelt, continued prayer makes tremendous power available—dynamic in its working. Father, I live in You—abide vitally united to You—and Your words remain in me and continue to live in my heart. When I produce much fruit, it brings great glory to my Father—the Father of my Lord Jesus Christ. Amen. (Add your personal daily prayer requests)

SCRIPTURE REFERENCES

- Luke 18:1
- Romans 8:26-28
- Mark 11:22-24
- James 5:13-18
- John 15:7-8

*I'll run the course You lay out for me
If You'll just show me how. God, teach me
Lessons for living so I can stay the course.
Give me insight so I can do what
You tell me my whole life...
One long, obedient response.*

Psalm 119:32-34

To Walk in God's Wisdom and His Perfect Will

Father, I ask You to give me a complete understanding of what You want to do in my life, and I ask You to make me wise with spiritual wisdom. Then, the way I live will always honor and please You, and I will continually do good, kind things for others. All the while, I will learn to know You better and better.

I roll my works upon You, Lord, and You make my thoughts agreeable to Your will, so my plans are established and will succeed. You direct my steps and make them sure. I understand and firmly grasp what the will of the Lord is for I am not vague, thoughtless, or foolish. I stand firm and mature in spiritual growth, convinced and fully assured in everything willed by God.

Father, You have destined and appointed me to come progressively to know Your will—that is to perceive, to recognize more strongly and clearly, and to become better and more intimately acquainted with Your will. I thank You, Father, for the Holy Spirit Who abides permanently in me and Who guides me into all the Truth—the whole, full Truth—and speaks whatever He hears from the Father and announces and declares to me the things that are to come. I have the mind of Christ and hold the thoughts, feelings, and purposes of His heart.

So, Father, I have entered into that blessed rest by adhering to, trusting in, and relying on You, as I acknowledge You in all of my ways, You are directing my paths. I believe that as I trust in You completely, You will show me the path of life, in the name of Jesus, Amen.

SCRIPTURE REFERENCES

- Ephesians 1:17-19
- Proverbs 3:5-6
- Colossians 1:9-14
- Acts 22:14
- Colossians 4:12

*My son, if you accept My words and store up
My commands within you, turning your ear to wisdom
And applying your heart to understanding, and if you
Call out for insight and cry aloud for understanding,
And if you look for it as for silver and search for it as for
Hidden treasure, then you will understand the fear
Of the Lord and find the knowledge of God.*

Proverbs 2:1-5

Godly Wisdom in the Affairs of Life

Father, You said if anyone lacks wisdom, let him ask of You, and it shall be given him. Therefore, I ask in faith, nothing wavering, to be filled with the knowledge of Your will in all wisdom and spiritual understanding. Today I incline my ear unto wisdom, and I apply my heart to understanding so that I might receive that which has been freely given unto me.

In the name of Jesus, I receive skill and Godly wisdom and instruction. I discern and comprehend the words of understanding and insight. I receive instruction in wise dealing and the discipline of wise thoughtfulness, righteousness, justice, and integrity. Prudence, knowledge, discretion, and discernment are given to me. I increase in knowledge. As a person of understanding, I acquire skill and attain to sound counsels so that I may be able to steer my course rightly.

Therefore, I will walk in paths of uprightness. When I walk, my steps shall not be hampered—my path will be clear and open; and when I run, I shall not stumble. I take fast hold of instruction and do not let her go; I guard her, for she is my life. I let my eyes look right on, with fixed purpose, and my gaze is straight before me. I consider well the path of my feet, and let all my ways be established and ordered aright.

Father, in the name of Jesus, I look carefully to how I walk! I live purposefully and worthily and accurately, not as unwise and witless, but as a wise—sensible, intelligent—person, making the very most of my time—buying up every opportunity. In Jesus' name. Amen.

SCRIPTURE REFERENCES

- Proverbs 4:11-12
- Proverbs 9:10-11
- James 1:5
- Colossians 2:3
- Proverbs 8:11

But if anyone does not provide for his own,
And especially for those of his household,
He has denied the faith,
And is worse than an unbeliever.

1 Timothy 5:8

FAMILY SECOND

*A man must leave his father and mother
When he marries, so that he can be perfectly joined
To his wife, and the two shall be one.*

Ephesians 5:31

My Wife and Marriage

Father, in the beginning, You provided a partner for man. Now I have found a wife to be my partner, and I have obtained favor from the Lord.

In the name of Jesus, I purpose to provide leadership to my wife the way Christ does to His church, not by domineering, but by cherishing. I will go all out in my love for her, exactly as Christ did for the Church—a love marked by giving, not getting. We are the Body of Christ, and when I love my wife, I love myself.

It is my desire to give my wife what is due her, and I purpose to share my personal rights with her. Father, I am neither anxious nor intimidated, but I am a good husband to my wife. I honor her and delight in her. In the new life of God's Grace, we are equals. I purpose to treat my wife as an equal so that our prayers will be answered.

We bear up under anything and everything that comes. We are ever ready to believe the best of each other. Our hopes are fadeless under all circumstances. We endure everything without weakening. Our love never fails—it never fades out or becomes obsolete or comes to an end.

We are no longer children tossed to and fro, carried about with every wind of doctrine, but we speak the truth in love, dealing truly and living truly. We are enfolded in love, growing up in every way and in all things. We esteem and delight in one another, forgiving one another readily and freely as God in Christ has forgiven us. We are imitators of God and copy His example as well-beloved children imitate their father.

Thank You, Father, that our marriage grows stronger each day because it is founded on Your Word and on Your kind of love. We give You the praise for it all, Father, in the name of Jesus, Amen. (Add any specific prayers you have for your wife.)

SCRIPTURE REFERENCES

- Genesis 2:18
- Proverbs 18:22
- 1 Peter 3:7
- Ephesians 5:22-31
- 1 Corinthians 7:3-5

*Houses and wealth are inherited from parents
But a prudent wife is from the Lord.*

Proverbs 19:14

Single Male Trusting God for a Mate

Father, in the name of Jesus, I believe that You are providing a suitable helpmate for me. According to Your Word, she will adapt herself to me, respect, honor, prefer, esteem me and stand firmly by my side. She will be united in spirit and purpose, having the same love and being in full accord and of one harmonious mind and intention.

Father, You say in Your Word that a wise, understanding, and prudent wife is from You. He who finds a true wife finds a good thing and obtains favor from You.

Father, I know that I have found favor in Your sight, and I praise You and thank You for Your Word, knowing that You watch over it to perform it. In Jesus' name, Amen.

SCRIPTURE REFERENCES

- Ephesians 5:21-33
- Proverbs 31:10,30
- 2 Corinthians 6:14-15

DAILY PRAYERS

Children are a gift from God; they are His reward.
Children born to a young man are like sharp
Arrows To defend him. Happy is the man who
Has his quiver full of them. That man shall have
The help he needs when arguing with his enemies.

Psalm 127:3-5

My Children

Father, in the name of Jesus, I pray and confess Your Word over my children, _____, and surround them with my faith—faith in Your Word that You watch over it to perform it! I confess and believe that my children are Disciples of Christ, taught of the Lord and obedient to Your will. Great is the peace and undisturbed composure of my children, because You, God, contend with that which contends with my children, and You give them safety and ease them.

Father, you will perfect that which concerns me. I commit that all may be well with my children and that they may live long on earth, for You are their Life and the Length of their days. I cast the care of my children once and for all over on You, Father. They are in Your hands, and I am positively persuaded that You are able to guard and keep that which I have committed to You. You are more than enough!

I believe and confess that You give Your angels charge over my children to accompany and defend and preserve them in all their ways. You, Lord, are their Refuge and Fortress. You protect them from the enemy. You are their Glory and the Lifter of their heads.

As a father, I will not provoke, irritate, or fret my children. I will not be hard on them or harass them or cause them to become discouraged, sullen, or morose, or to feel inferior and frustrated. I will not break or wound their spirits, but I will rear them tenderly in the training, discipline, counsel, and admonition of the Lord. I will train them in the way they should go, and when they are old, they will not depart from it. Thank you, Father, for caring for my children. In Jesus' name, Amen. (Add any specific prayers you may have for your children.)

SCRIPTURE REFERENCES

- Deuteronomy 6:6-7
- Isaiah 54:13
- Isaiah 49:25
- Ephesians 6:4
- Proverbs 22:6
- Proverbs 19:18
- Colossians 3:21
- Psalm 127:3-5

The generation of the upright will be blessed.
Wealth and riches are in His house,
And His righteousness endures forever.

Psalm 112:2-3

Blessing the Household

Father, as the priest and head of this household, I declare and decree, "As for me and my house, we shall serve the Lord."

Lord, we acknowledge and welcome the presence of Your Holy Spirit here in our home. We thank You Father, that Your Son, Jesus, is here with us because we are gathered together in His name.

As spiritual leader of this home, I declare on the authority of Your Word that my family will be mighty in the land; this generation of the upright will be blessed.

Father, You delight in the prosperity of Your people and we thank You for the blessings in our house and that our righteousness endures forever, in the name of Jesus, Amen.

SCRIPTURE REFERENCES

- Revelation 1:6
- Joshua 24:15
- Ephesians 1:3
- Psalm 112:1-3
- Psalm 128

DAILY PRAYERS

And God is able to make all grace abound to you,
So that in all things at all times,
Having all that you need, you will abound
In every good work. As it is written:
"He has scattered abroad His gifts to the poor;
His righteousness endures forever."

2 Corinthians 9:8-9

Handling Household Finances

Jesus, you are my Lord and my High Priest, and I purpose to bring You the first fruits of my income and worship You, the Lord my God, with them. Therefore, I believe in the name of Jesus that all my needs are met, according to Your riches in glory. I acknowledge You as Lord over my finances by giving tithes and offerings to further Your cause.

If you have not been giving tithes and offerings, include the following in your prayer: Forgive me for robbing you in the tithes and offerings. I repent and purpose to bring all my tithes into the storehouse that there may be food in your house. Thank you for wise financial counselors and teachers who are teaching me the principles of good stewardship.

Father, on the authority of Your Word, I declare that gifts will be given to me; good measure, pressed down, shaken together, and running over shall they be poured into my bosom. For with the same measure I deal out, it shall be measured back to me.

I remember that it is written in Your Word that he who sows sparingly and grudgingly, will also reap sparingly and grudgingly. He who sows generously that blessings may come to someone, will also reap generously and with blessings.

Father, not only do I give tithes and offerings to You, but I also give to those around me who are in need. Your Word also says that he who gives to the poor lends to You, and You pay wonderful interest on the loan! I acknowledge You as I give for the benefit of the poor.

Thank You, Father, that as You bless me and I bless others, they will praise You and give You thanks. They will bless others and the circle of Your love and blessings will go on and on into eternity, in the name of Jesus, Amen. (Add specific prayers for your own financial needs.)

SCRIPTURE REFERENCES

- Malachi 3:8-10
- Proverbs 3:9-10
- Proverbs 19:17
- 2 Corinthians 9:6-13
- Philippians 4:19
- Luke 6:38

DAILY PRAYERS

I will instruct you and teach you in the way
You should go; I will counsel you and
Watch over you.

Psalm 32:8

CAREER
THIRD

Whatever you do, work at it with all your heart,
As working for the Lord, not for men, since you know that
You will receive an inheritance from the Lord as a reward.
It is the Lord Christ you are serving.

Colossians 3:23-24

The Setting of Proper Priorities

Father, too often I allow urgency to dictate my schedule, and I am asking You to help me establish priorities in my work. My desire is to live purposefully, worthily, accurately as a wise, sensible, intelligent person.

You have given me a seven-day week—six days to work and the seventh day to rest. I desire to make the most of the time buying up each opportunity. Help me plan my day, and stay focused on my assignments. Help me to organize my efforts, schedule my activities and budget my time.

By the grace given me, I will not worry about missing out, and my everyday human concerns will be met. I purpose in my heart to seek first of all Your Kingdom, Lord, and Your righteousness, and then all things taken together will be given me.

Father, Your Word is my compass, and it helps me see my life as complete in Christ. I cast all my cares, worries and concerns on You, that I might be well-balanced, temperate, sober of mind, vigilant and cautious at all times.

Father, You sent Jesus that I might have life and have it more abundantly. Help me remember that my relationship with You and with others are more important than anything else. In the name of Jesus. Amen.

SCRIPTURE REFERENCES

- Ephesians 5:15-16
- Proverbs 16:3
- Matthew 11:28-30
- Psalm 37:3-5
- 1 Peter 5:5-9
- Mathew 6:25-34
- Exodus 20:9-11

DAILY PRAYERS

But remember the Lord your God,
For it is He who gives you the ability to produce wealth,
And so confirms His covenant,
Which He swore to your forefathers, as it is today.

Deuteronomy 8:18

Prayer for the Success
of Business (Only if you are self employed)

Father, I commit my works (the plans and cares of my business) to You, I entrust them wholly to You. Since You are effectually at work in me, You cause my thoughts to become agreeable with Your will, so that my business plans shall be established and will succeed. In the name of Jesus, I submit to every kind of wisdom, practical insight, and prudence, which You have lavished upon me in accordance with the riches and generosity of Your gracious favor.

Father, I affirm that I obey Your Word by making an honest living with my own hands, so that I may be able to give to those in need. In Your strength and according to Your grace, I provide for myself and my own family. Thank You, Father, for making all grace, every favor and earthly blessing, come to me in abundance that I, having all sufficiency may abound to every good work.

Thank You for the grace to remain diligent in seeking knowledge and skill in areas where I am inexperienced. I ask You for wisdom and the ability to understand righteousness, justice, and fair dealing in every area and relationship. I affirm that I am faithful and committed to Your Word. My life and business are founded upon its principles.

Father, thank You for the success of my business! In Jesus' name, Amen.

SCRIPTURE REFERENCES

- Psalm 1
- Luke 19:12-27
- Proverbs 22:29
- Proverbs 3:9-10
- Proverbs 27:23-27

If you're a hard worker and do a good job,
You deserve your pay; we don't call your wages a gift.
But if you see that the job is too big for you,
That it's something only God can do,
And you trust Him to do it, you could never
Do it for yourself, no matter how hard and long
You worked. Well, that trusting-Him-to-do-it is what
Gets you set right with God by God. Sheer gift.

Romans 4:4-5

Prayer for Personal Productivity on the Job

(If you are employed)

Father, I ask for Your help in planning my day, paying attention to my duties, staying focused on my assignment, establishing priorities in my work, and making steady progress toward my objectives.

Give me insight, Father. Help me to see any habits that I may have that might tend to make me nonproductive. Reveal to me ways to better handle the tedious tasks I must perform so that I can achieve the greatest results possible. Help me to organize my efforts, schedule my activities, and budget my time.

From books, by Your Spirit, through the people who work with me or by whatever means You choose, Lord, reveal to me that which I need to know and do in order to become a more productive, fruitful worker.

My heart's desire is to give my very best to You and to my employer. When I become frustrated because that is not taking place, help me, Father by the power of Your Spirit to do whatever is necessary to correct that situation so that I can once again function with accuracy and proficiency.

Thank You, Lord, for bringing all these things to pass in my life. In Jesus' name I pray, Amen. *(Add specific prayers for your personal challenges.)*

SCRIPTURE REFERENCES

- Colossians 3:23-24
- 3 John 1:2
- Galatians 6:9-10
- 1 Corinthians 15:58

DAILY PRAYERS

Watch the way you talk...
Say only what helps, each word a gift...
Be gentle with one another, sensitive.
Forgive one another as quickly and thoroughly
As God in Christ forgave you.

Ephesians 4:29, 32

Improving Communication Skills

Father, I am Your child, Jesus said that if I pray to You in secret, You will reward me openly. Show "me" to me. Uncover me and bring everything to the light. When anything is exposed by the light, it is made visible and clear; and where everything is visible and clear, there is light.

Teach me to speak the truth in love in my home, in my church, with my friends, and in all my relationships. Words are powerful. The power of life and death is in the tongue, and You said that I would eat the fruit of it. Father, I realize that words can be creative or destructive. A word out of my mouth may seem of no account, but it can accomplish nearly anything — or destroy it.

With the help of the Holy Spirit and by Your grace, I will not let any unwholesome talk come out of my mouth, but only what is helpful for building others up according to their needs, that it may benefit those who listen, in Jesus' name, Amen.

SCRIPTURE REFERENCES

- Ephesians 4:15,29
- Ephesians 5:1-14
- Psalm 45:1-2
- Proverbs 8:6-8
- Proverbs 10:20-21

DAILY PRAYERS

The first thing I want you to do is pray.
Pray every way you know how, for everyone you know.
Pray especially for rulers and their governments
To rule well so we can be quietly about our business
Of living simply, in humble contemplation.
This is the way our Savior God wants us to live.

1 Timothy 2:1-3

Prayer for the President and Our Nation

Father, in Jesus' name, I give thanks for the United States and its government. I hold up in prayer before You the men and women who are in positions of authority.

I pray that skillful and Godly wisdom will enter into the heart of our President and knowledge is pleasant to him. May discretion watch over him; may understanding keep him and deliver him from the way of evil and from evil men.

Your Word declares that "blessed is the nation whose God is the Lord." We receive Your blessing. Father, You are our Refuge and Stronghold. I declare that Your people dwell safely in this land, and prosper abundantly. We are all more than conquerors through Christ Jesus!

It is written in Your Word that the heart of our President is in the hand of the Lord and that You turn it whichever way You desire. I pray that You put the heart of our President in Your hands Father, and from this day forward that all his decisions will be divinely directed by You.

I give thanks unto You that the good news of the Gospel is published in our land. I pray that The Word of the Lord prevails and grows mightily in the hearts and lives of the American people. I give thanks for this land and the leaders You have given to us, in Jesus' name I pray, Amen.

SCRIPTURE REFERENCES

- 1 Timothy 2:1-3
- Psalm 9:9
- Psalm 33:12
- Deuteronomy 28:10-11
- Romans 8:37
- Proverbs 21:1

DAILY PRAYERS

It is good to praise the Lord and make music to Your Name,
O Most High, to proclaim Your love in the morning
And your faithfulness at night.

Psalm 92:1-2

To Glorify God

In view of God's mercy, I offer my body as a living sacrifice, holy and pleasing to God—this is my spiritual act of worship. It is not in my own strength; for it is You, Lord, who are all the while effectually at work in me. You are energizing and creating in me the power and desire—both to will and work for Your good pleasure and satisfaction and delight.

Father, I will not draw back or shrink in fear, for then Your soul would have no delight or pleasure in me. I was bought for a price—purchased with a preciousness and paid for, made Your very own. So, then, I honor You Lord, and bring glory to You in my body. I called on You in the day of trouble; You delivered me. I shall honor and glorify You. I rejoice because You delivered me and drew me to Yourself. You took me out of the control and dominion of darkness, obscurity, and transferred me into the Kingdom of the Son of Your love. I will confess and praise You, O Lord my God, with my whole, united heart. I will glorify Your name forever.

As a bond servant of Jesus Christ, I receive and develop the talents that have been given me, for I would have You say of me, "Well done, you upright and faithful servant!" I make use of the gifts (faculties, talents, qualities) according to the grace given me. I let my light shine before men that they may see my moral excellence and my praiseworthy, noble and good deeds. I recognize, honor, praise and glorify my Father Who is in heaven.

In the name of Jesus, I allow my life to lovingly express truth in all things— speaking truly, dealing truly and living truly. Whatever I do, no matter what it is—in word or deed, I do everything in the name of the Lord Jesus Christ. My dependence is upon His Person, giving praise to God the Father through Him.

Whatever may be my task, I work at it heartily from the soul, as something done for the Lord and not for men. To God the Father be all glory, honor and praise. In the name of Jesus. Amen.

SCRIPTURE REFERENCES

- Romans 12:1-6
- Philippians 2:13
- Matthew 25:14-30

NOTES

NOTES

NOTES

NOTES